Survivor's Science on an
Island

Peter D. Riley

HODDER
Wayland

An imprint of Hodder Children's Books

© 2003 White-Thomson Publishing Ltd

White-Thomson Publishing Ltd,
2-3 St Andrew's Place, Lewes,
East Sussex BN7 1UP

Published in Great Britain in 2003 by Hodder
Wayland, an imprint of Hodder Children's
Books

This book was produced for White-Thomson
Publishing Ltd by Ruth Nason.

Design and illustration: Carole Binding

The right of Peter D. Riley to be identified as
the author of this work has been asserted by
him in accordance with the Copyright,
Designs and Patents Act 1988.

British Library Cataloguing in Publication Data
Peter D. Riley
    On An Island. - (Survivor's Science)
    1. Island ecology - Juvenile literature
    I. Title
    577.5'2

ISBN 0 7502 4237 X

Printed in Hong Kong

Hodder Children's Books
A division of Hodder Headline Limited
338 Euston Road, London NW1 3BH

Acknowledgements
The author and publishers thank the following for their permission to
reproduce photographs: Corbis: pages 1 and 13 (M. Dillon), 4 (Bill Ross), 6t
and 11t (Jim Sugar Photography), 8 (Yann Arthus-Bertrand), 16l (Richard
Hamilton Smith), 20 (Wolfgang Kaehler), 24t (Robert van der Hilst), 26 (Sergio
Pitamitz), 29 (Jack Fields), 34 (Dennis Degnan), 36 (Catherine Karnow), 40
(Mark A. Johnson), 44 (Wolfgang Kaehler); Ecoscene: page 7 (Sally Morgan);
Science Photo Library: pages 11 (Jeremy Bishop), 12 (Michael McCoy), 18b (Dr
Jeremy Burgess), 24b (David Nunuk), 37 (Lynette Cook); Still Pictures: pages
6bl and 30 (Kjell B. Sandved), 6br and 18 and cover (Jany Sauvenet), 15 and
cover (Truchet-UNEP), 16r (Julia Baine), 22 (Norbert Wu), 25 (Andre
Maslennikov), 33 (Gerard & Margi Moss), 38 (Rebecca Mills-Christian Aid), 42
(Alan Watson). The science activity photographs are by Carole Binding.

Contents

Introduction

Sometimes people describe islands as 'desert islands'. The name comes from the word 'deserted', which means uninhabited or left to grow wild.

What is an island?

An island is a piece of land that is surrounded by water. This could be a lake or the sea. In this book we are going to look at survival on a particular kind of island in the sea.

Islands in the sea may form in many ways. Some are made when sand builds up into a huge bank that rises above the water. Others are created when parts of a coastline are washed away by the sea, leaving land cut off from the shore. But the islands we are going to visit have formed from volcanoes, in the warmer seas of the world.

Once a volcano has made the island, the island's size is increased as coral grows around its shores. Scientists find these islands particularly interesting because of the range of things to study on them.

The keys to survival

In mainland places people can travel a long way overland to gather the things they need to survive. On an island, it is not so easy for people to fetch what they need from far away. They have to learn to survive by using just the things they can find on the island. Many small islands cannot provide enough food and materials for human survival and they are uninhabited. But larger islands can provide all the needs for survival, and people have been living on some of them for thousands of years.

Explorers make **expeditions** onto the islands to study volcanoes and the rocks from which the islands are made. Others go to investigate the way the coral is growing, or to find out about the plants and animals that have set up home on the islands. Before an expedition, the explorers plan how they will survive. They study what to wear, how to travel safely, how to find the way, how to make a shelter, how to stay healthy, and, if there is an emergency, how to be rescued.

Discovering with science

For thousands of years people have investigated their surroundings and made discoveries that have helped them survive. About 400 years ago, a way of investigating called the scientific method was devised, to help us understand our world more clearly. The main features of the scientific method are:

1 Making an **observation**

2 Thinking of an idea to explain the observation

3 Doing a test or experiment to test the idea

4 Looking at the result of the test and comparing it with the idea

Today the scientific method is used to provide explanations for almost everything. In this book you can find out about the science that helps people, plants and animals survive on islands – particularly those in warm seas. You can also try some activities to see how different areas of science, such as the study of materials and the weather, help us understand how people can survive where there are few resources. In these activities you may use the whole of the scientific method or just parts of it, such as making observations or doing experiments. But you will always be using science to make discoveries.

Are you ready to find out how people can survive on an island? Turn the page to find the major groups of islands in the warmer parts of the world's oceans and seas.

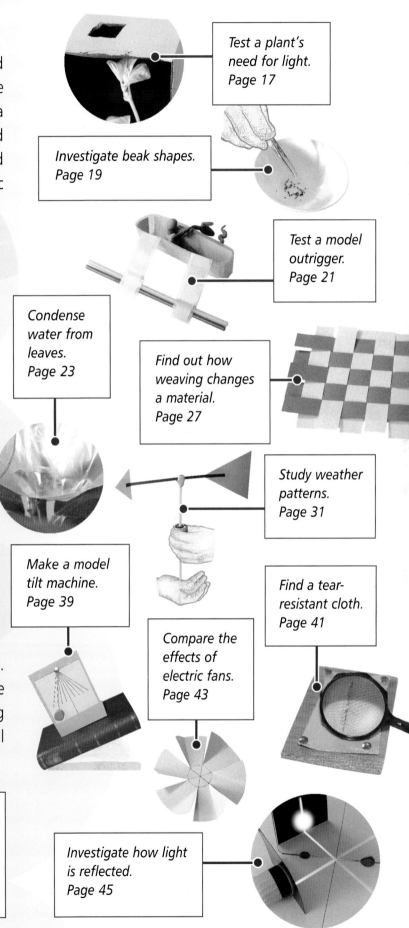

Test a plant's need for light.
Page 17

Investigate beak shapes.
Page 19

Test a model outrigger.
Page 21

Condense water from leaves.
Page 23

Find out how weaving changes a material.
Page 27

Study weather patterns.
Page 31

Make a model tilt machine.
Page 39

Find a tear-resistant cloth.
Page 41

Compare the effects of electric fans.
Page 43

Investigate how light is reflected.
Page 45

Warm-water islands

The Hawaiian Islands

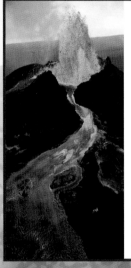

These islands have several **active** volcanoes.

One plant here is the candle nut tree. The nut oil is used to make candles. Many kinds of birds called honeycreepers live on the islands.

The islands of the Caribbean Sea

A plant called aloe vera grows on the drier parts of these islands. Part of the food that it makes for itself is in the form of an oil. The plant is grown as a crop, and its oil is used to make cosmetics.

The coney is an animal like a guinea pig. It is in danger of **extinction**.

Bermuda

There are many flowering plants on Bermuda including the Easter lily.

The cahow is a pigeon-like bird with a wing span of nearly 1 metre.

Tropic of Cancer

Pacific Ocean

Atlantic Ocean

Bahamas

Caribbean Sea

Barbados

Jamaica

Solomon Is.

Equator

Tropic of Capricorn

Easter Is.

Fiji

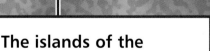

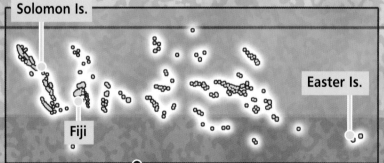

The islands of the South Pacific Ocean

The coconut palm is a common plant on these islands. A common animal is the fruit bat.

The Galapagos Islands

These islands are home to the Galapagos tree fern and about 15,000 giant tortoises.

The islands of the Indian Ocean

Comoros
A type of fish called the coelacanth was believed to have been extinct for 70 million years. Then, about 50 years ago, scientists found coelacanth living in the waters around the Comoros. Local people had caught the fish and known about them well before that time.

Mauritius
The echo parakeet and the pink pigeon are two rare birds found on this island. It was also home to the dodo, a bird that is now extinct. The dodo tree has silver bark and brown seeds.

Seychelles
The coco de mer is one of many kinds of coconut palm that grow on the Seychelles. It produces the largest seeds on Earth. About 20,000 giant tortoises live on one of the islands, Aldabra.

All the groups of islands shown here are made from the tops of underwater mountains. All are made from volcanoes and coral, except for the Seychelles. The largest islands in the Seychelles group are made out of **granite**. The others in the group are made from coral. The type of coral that forms islands only grows in warm water. That is why all these islands are near the equator.

When an island forms, it is not long before plants and animals arrive from other places. Each island group has some plants and animals that are found nowhere else. Scientists believe that the ancestors of these living things came from other lands but, as they bred on the island, each generation changed slightly until a new **species** formed. Some of these unusual plants and animals are mentioned here.

The first people on the Earth lived on the large areas of land called continents. Eventually people sailed along the coasts of the continents to fish and to trade. Some began to explore the oceans and discovered the island groups.

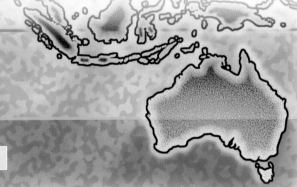

Seychelles

Comoros

Mauritius

Indian Ocean

The Tropics

The largest areas of water, between the continents, are called oceans. Areas of salt water closer to the land, or partly or completely surrounded by land, are called seas.

They set up home on the larger islands, where they could find enough food and water. Sometimes crops such as sugar cane were planted for food and for trade. Today, people from many parts of the world may live on one island. For example, on the Caribbean islands, there are people from Africa, Europe, India and the USA.

How volcanoes make islands

This island formed from a volcano is part of the Galapagos group. These islands are about 1,000 km west of the South American mainland.

The power to make islands rise out of the sea starts thousands of kilometres below the seabed – at the centre or core of the Earth. It is thought that changes take place in **radioactive substances** at the core, and during the changes large amounts of heat are released. This heat passes from the core towards the Earth's surface.

The structure of the Earth is divided into four parts. They are the inner and outer core, the mantle and the crust. The mantle is made of solid rock, but the heat from the core softens it a little and makes it flow like toothpaste when you slowly squeeze the tube. The heat is carried towards the surface by the slow movements of rock in the mantle.

A cross section of the Earth

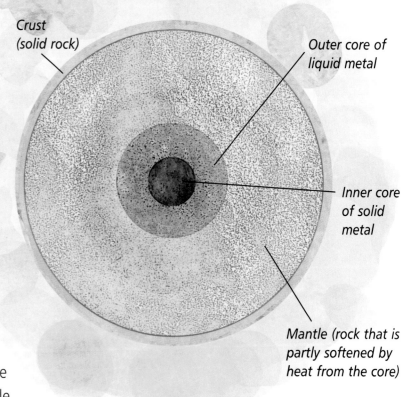

Crust (solid rock)

Outer core of liquid metal

Inner core of solid metal

Mantle (rock that is partly softened by heat from the core)

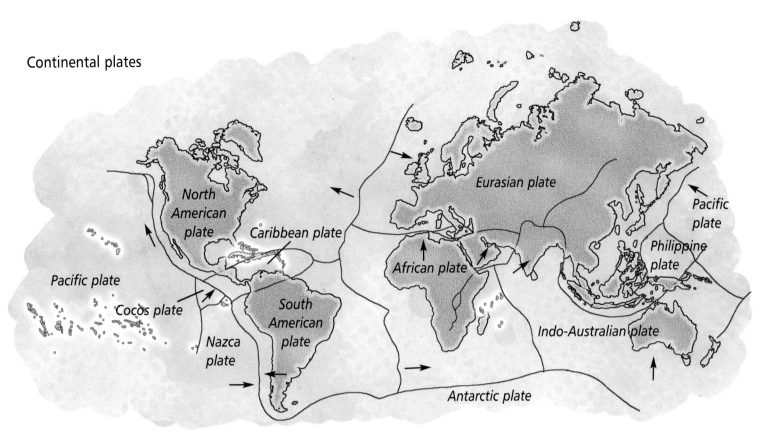

Continental plates

North American plate
Caribbean plate
Pacific plate
Cocos plate
Nazca plate
South American plate
Eurasian plate
Pacific plate
Philippine plate
African plate
Indo-Australian plate
Antarctic plate

The Earth's crust is not one huge piece of rock. It is made from large slabs of rock called **plates**. The plates rest on the hot surface of the mantle, and where the mantle moves, the plates move too. In some places the plates move apart. In others they crash into each other.

Where volcanoes form

A volcano is a crack in the Earth's crust through which **molten** rock, ash and gases pass. The molten rock is called **magma**. Volcanoes can form where the Earth's plates move apart, or where they crash together and one is pushed under another. Volcanoes also form above 'hot spots' on the surface of the Earth's mantle. These are regions of the mantle that are always very hot. Heat and magma pass into the crust above them.

If a volcano forms under the sea, it may eventually become so large that it breaks through the water surface and becomes an island. Sometimes several volcanic islands form in a line. This happens where an island appears above a 'hot spot'. Because the Earth's plates are slowly moving, the island gradually moves away from the 'hot spot'. Then a nearby part of the Earth's crust is affected by the hot spot, and a new volcanic island forms. Again, this second island moves away and a third island begins to form, and so on.

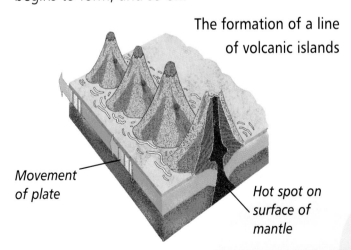

The formation of a line of volcanic islands

Movement of plate

Hot spot on surface of mantle

Volcanic islands do not only form in warm seas. They also form in cold ones. Surtsey is a volcanic island, which formed in the North Atlantic in 1963.

What is inside a volcano?

Inside a volcano there is a space where magma collects. The magma may be thin and runny or thick and slow-moving, but there is always a mixture of gases dissolved in it. When the space or 'magma chamber' is full, the magma pushes its way out of the volcano's **vent** and an **eruption** takes place.

When no more hot rock comes to fill its magma chamber, the volcano is called 'extinct'. The chamber may collapse, and the top of the volcano may form a **crater**.

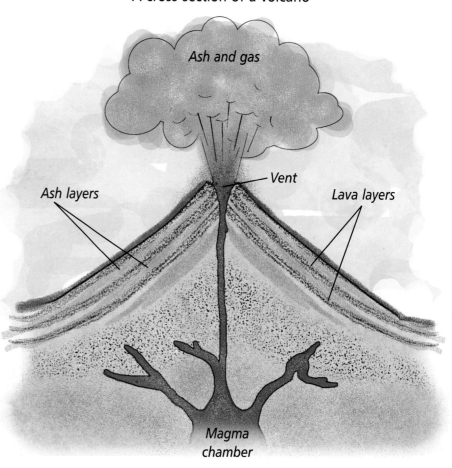

A cross section of a volcano

Ash and gas

Vent

Ash layers

Lava layers

Magma chamber

Volcano shapes

The magma that flows out of an erupting volcano is called lava. As it cools, it becomes solid rock.

The shape of a volcano depends on whether the lava is thin or thick. When thin, runny lava pours from a volcano's vent, the gases in it escape gradually and make only small explosions. The runny lava travels a long way before it cools and becomes solid. Gradually, over many eruptions, runny lava makes a volcano with gently sloping sides. This shape is called a 'shield volcano'.

Thicker lava does not travel far before it becomes solid. This slow-moving lava gradually makes a volcano with steep sides and a cone shape.

Ash, blocks and bombs

There is great danger as gas escapes quickly from thick, slow-moving lava. At first it forms bubbles in the lava. Then these bubbles crack open, causing violent explosions.

The explosions shoot particles of rock into the air. The smallest particles are less than 4 millimetres across and are called ash. Particles over 32 millimetres across are called 'blocks' and 'bombs'. Blocks are pieces of rock that were solid when they were shot into the air. Bombs are lumps of molten rock. They change their shape as they fly through the air and may look like lemons or loaves of bread before they hit the ground. A big explosion from a cone-shaped volcano can cause great devastation.

Are all volcanoes dangerous?

Volcanoes may be active, **dormant** or extinct. All active volcanoes are dangerous, but some are more dangerous than others. When a shield volcano erupts, it may be watched from a safe distance. When a cone-shaped volcano erupts, you may have to run for your life. When a volcano becomes extinct, it is safe.

 Lava bursts from a volcano on one of the Hawaiian Islands. The volcanoes in these islands are a main tourist attraction.

 Scientists getting close to an erupting volcano need special protective clothing.

Dressing for the volcano

A volcanologist is a scientist who studies volcanoes. Some volcanologists try to get very close to lava, to take samples and measure temperatures. They wear a hard hat to protect them from blocks and bombs and a suit coated in shiny metal to protect them from the great heat. This coating reflects most of the heat that strikes it and keeps the volcanologist cool. However, the suit does not allow the volcanologist to move freely. If an eruption suddenly increased, the volcanologist may not be able to move fast enough to get away.

A coral island

Coral is a rocky substance made by some animals that belong to the jellyfish group. All coral-making animals have a body shape called a polyp. The polyp has a small and cylindrical body, with a mouth and ring of **tentacles** at one end. At the other end of the body, the animal is joined to the bodies of other coral animals. Many thousands of coral-making animals live together in a **colony**.

Coral branch

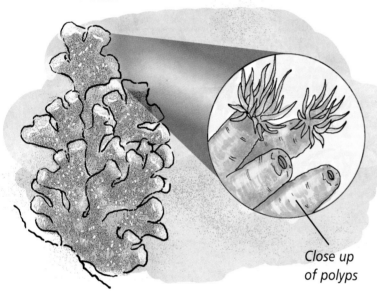

Close up
of polyps

Why coral is made

There is a substance called calcium, which is dissolved in seawater. The coral animals can take calcium out of the seawater and use it to make a rocky coating around themselves. This protects them from fish that might eat them. As many coral animals live together, the rocky coating of one sticks to the coating of another and the whole colony becomes covered in a lump of coral.

Coral gradually grows into a ridge below the water surface, called a coral reef. This is part of the coral reef around one of the Solomon Islands in the South Pacific Ocean.

An island may form when the top of a coral reef fills with sand. This example is in the Caribbean Sea.

How coral animals feed

There are holes in the lump of coral – one hole for each polyp. During the day the coral animals hide in their holes, but at night they extend their tentacles from the holes to catch tiny sea creatures for food. There are stingers on the tentacles, which **paralyse** the prey. Once the prey has stopped struggling, the tentacles push the prey into the mouth and it is **digested**. Each animal takes the food it needs and passes the rest to others in the colony. When the polyps are well fed, they produce lumps on their sides called 'buds'. These grow into new polyps, which in turn can make more coral.

From coral lump to island

Over time, a small piece of coral can grow into a huge ridge just below the water surface. This is called a **coral reef**. If the top of the reef fills with sand, a coral island can form – and coconut palms may grow on it.

Why coral islands are in warm seas

Coral polyps have plant-like **organisms**, called **algae**, living inside their bodies. The algae play an important part in the survival of the coral animals. They help the animals make coral from the calcium in the seawater. Algae make their own food, but they need plenty of sunlight and warmth to do it. This means they need clear, warm water. This kind of water is found in many warm seas of the world, where the water temperature never falls below 20ºC.

How a volcano and coral can make an island

Coral reefs need shallow water in which to grow. This may be off the coast of a continent. For example, the Great Barrier Reef lies off the coast of Australia. Shallow water is also found around an island formed by a volcano.

Once lava has stopped flowing into the sea, it is safe for coral animals to settle and begin to form colonies. These can grow all around the island and form a huge ring called a fringe reef.

The action of the waves breaks up dead coral and turns it into sand, which may form part of the beach on the island. There are also periods of wet and windy weather in the region where the islands form. These conditions break down the volcanic rocks in a process called **erosion**. This makes the volcano smaller.

If the volcano is extinct, no new rock is produced to replace the rock that is eroded. Eventually, the remains of the volcano sink beneath the sea surface. The coral continues to grow on its sides and forms a ring called an atoll. This may break up into a ring of coral islands.

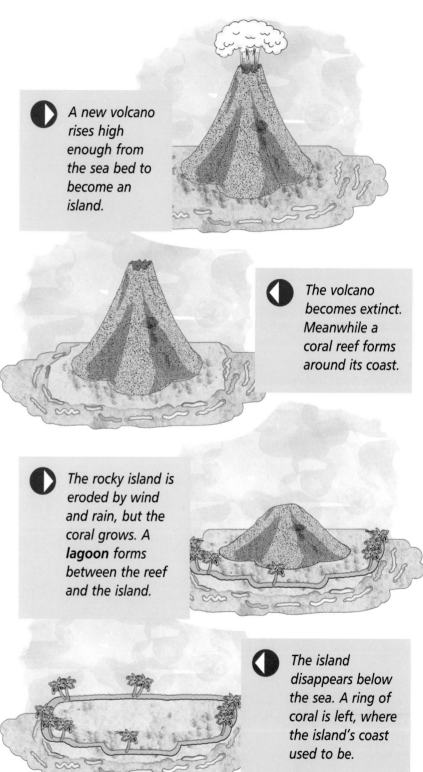

A new volcano rises high enough from the sea bed to become an island.

The volcano becomes extinct. Meanwhile a coral reef forms around its coast.

The rocky island is eroded by wind and rain, but the coral grows. A *lagoon* forms between the reef and the island.

The island disappears below the sea. A ring of coral is left, where the island's coast used to be.

Bora Bora, in the Pacific Ocean, is an example of a volcanic island. The coral reef around it has formed an atoll. The shallow water between the atoll and the island is called a lagoon.

Dangers on the coral reef

A coral reef provides a home for many other animals. Many are harmless, but some can be deadly. These animals are dangerous to humans, but people themselves are a danger to the coral-making animals. Coral animals have such delicate bodies that they die if they are touched. If the coral animals die, other animals living among the coral lose their homes and can die too.

The blue-ringed octopus

The blue-ringed octopus lives in crevices in a coral reef. At the centre of its tentacles, every octopus has a bird-like beak. If a blue-ringed octopus attacks you, it injects poison with its bite and this can kill.

The stone fish

The stone fish lives in crevices in the coral. It is highly **camouflaged**. It has poisonous spines on its back. If someone stands on a fish or puts their hand into a crevice, the poison may be injected into their skin. Stonefish poison can kill.

The cone shell

The cone shell is a type of sea snail. Inside, it has a hard, hollow structure called a tooth, which becomes filled with poison. When the cone shell finds its prey, it shoots the tooth into it like a harpoon. The poison quickly kills the prey so the cone shell can feed. Some cone shells have poisons strong enough to kill a human.

How plants reach a new island

On some tropical islands, plants grow into lush rainforest.

If seeds are brought to an area of volcanic soil, some will grow into plants.

When a new island forms from a volcano, the rocks are so hot that nothing can survive there at first. Eventually, the rock cools and gradually parts of it break up into small pieces and form soil. Once there is soil, seeds that arrive on the island may grow into plants.

Most plants make seeds and these may reach a new island in a number of ways. Some seeds have parachutes and are transported by the wind. Other seeds stick to the feet and feathers of birds, which carry them to the island. A few travel in the **digestive system** of birds and arrive on the island in a bird dropping, with their own ready-made **fertilizer**.

Some seeds travel across the sea on **driftwood**, but the salt water may kill them on their journey. Few plants can survive in salt water. The seeds of the coconut palm are unusual. They can float in seawater for thousands of kilometres and, when they are cast up on an island shore, they grow into palm trees there.

Most other plants can only survive away from the splashes of salt water and do not grow on the shore. They send their roots down into the soil and use rain water that has collected there. Most islands in warm oceans receive large amounts of rain and, if the island is large enough, a rainforest will form.

Can a plant find the light?

A plant needs water, warmth and light, to grow. But when a new plant starts to grow among many others (as in a rainforest), the taller plants block the light. You can make a model of these conditions, to see if a plant can find its way to the light.

You need a box with a lid, painted black inside, scissors, black card, sticky tape, a broad bean seed from a health food shop (this will not have **fungicide** on it), water, a small plant pot of **compost**.

1 Cut a hole of about 3cm² in one end of the box.

3cm² hole

2 Cut a piece of card to fit in the box, as shown in the photo. Tape the card in place.

3 Soak the seed in water overnight and let it swell up.

4 Plant the seed in the pot of compost and place this in the bottom of the box.

5 Put the box lid in place to close the open side.

6 Set the box in a warm, sunny place. Then check the pot every day and water the compost if it is dry. Draw or photograph the seedling as it tries to find the light.

7 Repeat the investigation with two cards arranged as in the bottom photograph. What do you find?

When animals reach an island

When an island forms, it is invaded by animals. Birds, bats and insects arrive by air. Young spiders hanging from a thread of silk may travel in the air, too. Rats, lizards and snakes may be carried to the island on logs that have floated away from a distant shore. Giant tortoises may arrive as they float from one island to another.

Many of the animals may not survive when they reach the island, because they cannot find food or shelter. So those that do survive have most of the island to themselves.

In places on continents, such as rainforests and woodland, many species of animals live together. Each species produces young, and some of the animals that are born may be a little different from the others in their species. For example, they may feed in a different way. These animals don't usually

Many species of animals and plants developed on the Galapagos Islands. These include several species of giant tortoise.

survive, because there are other species that already feed in that way and they get to the food first. But many scientists believe that, on an island, something unusual happens.

On a small island there are fewer species. So, when some young animals feed in a new way, they don't have to compete with other species to find food. Therefore they can survive, and pass on their way of feeding to their young. Over time, the animals with a different way of feeding become different in other ways too and a new species comes into being.

In the nineteenth century, the scientist Charles Darwin studied the wildlife on the Galapagos Islands. He noticed that different species of finches had developed, with different-shaped beaks.

Does the shape of a bird's beak affect how it feeds?

Scientists sometimes use models to help them in an investigation. In this investigation, the bird's beaks are models made from two pairs of forceps or tweezers.

You need two dishes, cress seeds, a stop clock or watch, a pair of pointed forceps, a pair of blunt forceps.

1 Put about 50 seeds in one dish, and place the empty dish close by it.

2 Set the stop clock or watch running for two minutes, while you use the blunt forceps to move as many seeds as you can into the empty dish. Make sure that you use the forceps in a pecking motion.

3 Count how many seeds you have moved and write it down.

4 Put all the seeds back into one dish and repeat steps 2 and 3, using the pointed forceps.

5 When scientists make an investigation, they repeat it a few times and compare their results. So repeat steps 1-4 twice more and compare your results. What do you find?

Conduct each experiment for two minutes.

How people came to the islands

Traditional sailing canoes are still used in the South Pacific.

How people came to the islands

People first set up home on the continents. They discovered islands when they began sailing, to catch fish or to carry goods for trade. At first, sailors stopped off at islands to collect fresh water and food. Later, people settled on larger islands, where there were enough resources to meet their needs all year round.

Islands close to the continents were discovered first. Then, as people built larger boats and learned more about how to travel across the oceans, they reached more distant islands. In the South Pacific Ocean, people used canoes up to 25 metres long. Some craft were made by joining two canoes together, side by side. Other craft had just one canoe and an outrigger. An outrigger is a long piece of wood attached to the side of a canoe and supported by a float. It helps prevent the canoe from overturning.

Cloth sails were used to catch the wind and drive the craft across the ocean at speeds of up to 250 kilometres a day. At these speeds, sailors could cover distances as great as 5,000 kilometres between islands before the food stored on board was all used up.

Some people have become interested in how these long journeys were made. They have made new canoes from old designs and used them to make the long journeys again, to see what it was like to try to survive them.

How does an outrigger help?

Many small boats in the South Pacific have outriggers. The boats are used to sail out from the island to fish. Make this model and test different materials for use as the outrigger.

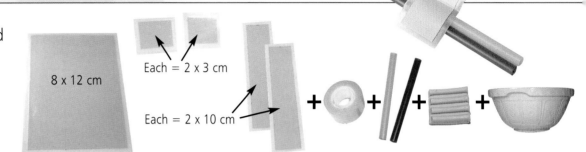

You need laminated card cut to the sizes shown, sticky tape, two straws, modelling clay, a bowl of water.

8 x 12 cm

Each = 2 x 3 cm

Each = 2 x 10 cm

1 Fold the large piece of laminated card along the lines shown on the right, to make the body of a model canoe. Tape the two smallest pieces of card in position, to make the ends of the canoe.

3cm 2cm 3cm

Fold pieces of card along these lines.

2 cm   5.5cm   2.5cm

2 Use the two long pieces of card to make the two arms of the outrigger. Tape them to the canoe.

3 Then tape the straws to the underside of the outrigger arms.

4 Make a person to sit in your canoe and float the craft in a bowl of water. Make some waves in the water to see how the outrigger supports the canoe.

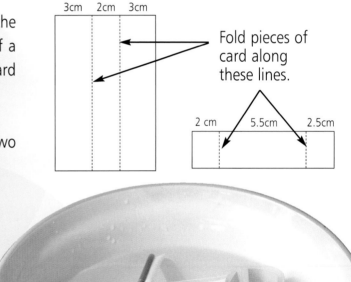

5 Use other materials to make the outrigger, such as different kinds of wooden rods (pencils), and make a fair test to compare them.

Finding water

Water is one of the most important things that people need in order to be able to survive in a place. Islands near the equator have wet weather at many times of year. Rainwater drains into the soil and rocks and is drawn up into the roots of plants that grow there. On large islands there may be streams and pools, but on small islands there may be none. One reason why many small islands are uninhabited is that they do not have a supply of water that people could use.

People who are shipwrecked and land on a desert island may need to collect water. One way is to arrange cloths, or the woven leaves of coconut palms, so that they catch rainwater and funnel it into a can. Another way is to **condense water vapour** as it escapes from the underside of leaves. The activity on page 23 shows how this is done.

A supply of water means that plants can grow and other living things have a chance of survival.

Steam   Pipe   *Distilled water condenses here*

Heat source   Salt is left behind   *Container of cold water keeps second container cool so that more steam condenses in it*

Distilling seawater

Seawater contains large amounts of salt. It must not be drunk, because the salt would damage many of the organs in the body and the person would die. However, people stranded on a desert island could **distil** seawater, to make it safe to drink. They would need to find fuel, such as wood, to make a fire, three containers and a tube. Seawater is boiled in one container. The water turns into steam, while the salt is left behind in the container. The steam passes through the tube and condenses in the second container. The condensed steam is water without salt. It may be drunk, if the second container is clean.

Can you condense water from leaves?

Water that is drawn from the soil into the roots of plants passes up through their stems and into the leaves, in a process called **transpiration**. Most of the water evaporates inside the leaves and changes to water vapour. On the underside of the leaves there are many microscopic holes, which open in the day and let the water vapour out. If this water vapour is made to condense, it forms liquid water again.

You need a tree growing outside, a clear plastic bag, a piece of string about 30cm long, a measuring cylinder.

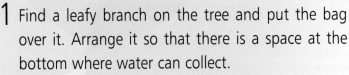

1 Find a leafy branch on the tree and put the bag over it. Arrange it so that there is a space at the bottom where water can collect.

2 Tie the bag firmly to the branch so that it is airtight and water vapour cannot escape from it.

3 Leave the bag for a few hours. Then measure how much water you have collected.

4 Does this method of collecting water work better on a dull day or a sunny day? Work out an experiment to find out.

Water collects in here.

Warning!

Do not drink the water you have collected. It may contain bacteria, which could make you ill.

Finding food

Fish is an important food for people who live on islands, like these men in the Comoros Islands.

The sea can provide food. At low tide, rock pools trap shrimps. These can be caught in nets and cooked on sticks over a fire.

Mussels and clams are kinds of shellfish called **bivalves**. They have two shells, which clamp over their body to give protection. Bivalves feed on tiny living things in seawater such as algae. Some algae that they take in at certain times of year contain poisons. For this reason the bivalves should only be gathered by local people, who know when it is safe to eat them.

Island people may dig for clams, which live buried in the sand. The two shells are split apart to reach the body of the creature.

Almost all desert islands have coconut palms growing on them. The coconut can provide a nutritious drink called milk, and a white solid food called meat. As a coconut develops, it changes from green to dark brown. People should avoid drinking the milk from very young green nuts and from old dark brown nuts, as it can give them diarrhoea. Also, the meat should only be eaten in small amounts, as the body cannot digest large quantities.

Sometimes other plants that grow with the coconut palms can provide fruit for food. These include screw pines, wild plums and passion fruit.

Large colonies of birds live on some islands. They make their nests there and rear their chicks. A hungry castaway could gather some eggs from the nests and cook them for a meal.

Fire

Fire is needed for boiling water and cooking food, such as shellfish and fish. If you land on an island without matches or a lighter, you can still get a fire going. Rubbing pieces of wood together can generate enough heat to start a fire. In Western Samoa, the wood of the hibiscus plant can be used to make a fire in seconds. A piece of the wood is laid on the ground and rubbed quickly backwards and forwards with a stick. A groove develops in the wood and wood powder collects at one end of it. The action of rubbing makes the wood become hot and the wood powder starts to glow. When small dry fibres from a coconut shell are placed near the glowing powder, they burst into flame and can be used to light a fire.

This woman in the Seychelles is cutting coconuts in half before leaving them to dry. Drying food helps to preserve it so it can be stored and used when other foods cannot be found.

The amount of wood on an island may be quite small, so it must be conserved to last a long time. One way to conserve wood when cooking is to set a fire going and cover it with volcanic rocks. The rocks take up heat from the flames and store it. Food wrapped in palm leaves can be placed on the rocks and covered with more palm leaves to keep in the heat. The heat from the rocks passes to the food and cooks it. The fire can be allowed to go out and wood can be saved for another time.

Using island materials

People need materials to help them survive. They need materials for building a shelter, making a fire, cooking, and storing food. A major problem if you are stranded on a small island is that the materials you find may soon run out. For example, if you use wood every day to make a fire to cook food, there may soon be no wood left. There's nowhere to go to find more wood.

On an island you must search the shore at low tide each day, to see if anything useful, such as driftwood, has been washed up. You must also learn how to use materials in different ways. For example, the long thin leaves of some of the plants on an island can be woven together, to make walls, baskets, mats and even hats to protect people from the Sun.

How weaving makes a strong material

If twelve long thin leaves are laid on top of another twelve leaves, at right angles, some of their surfaces touch and grip each other by **friction**. But if you shake them, they fall away from each other because the friction is weak.

Weaving the leaves together means bending them over and under each other. The leaves are springy, and this property makes them push on each other more strongly when they are woven. This increases the friction between them and helps to hold them in place. The way the leaves are woven also makes them interlock to give extra strength.

● *Driftwood washed up onto the beach by the tide could be useful for building a shelter or making a fire.*

Compare the strength

You can experiment with strips of cardboard, to find out the effect of weaving a material.

You need 2 rulers, 10 strips of cardboard 10cm long, a clock.

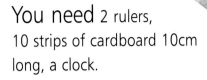

+ +

1 Place the rulers 8cm apart and rest 5 cardboard strips across them.

2 Place the other 5 strips across the first strips so that they are in line with the rulers.

3 Carefully pick up the rulers and gently bounce them up and down. Note what happens to the strips after 20 seconds.

4 Place 5 strips on the tabletop and weave one strip through as the photo shows.

5 Weave a second strip through.

6 Weave the third strip like the first, the fourth like the second, and the fifth like the first.

7 Rest the woven strips on the rulers and repeat step 3.

8 How does weaving affect the way the strips behave?

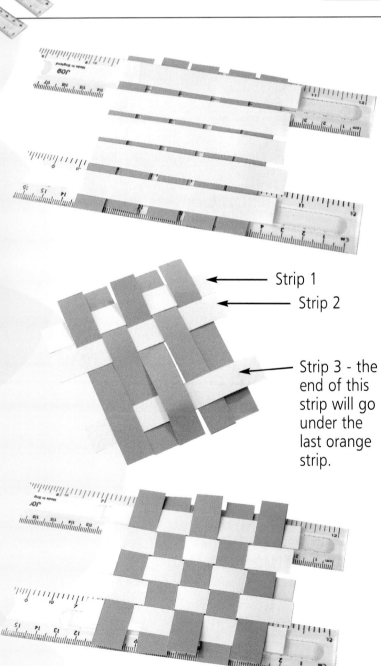

Strip 1

Strip 2

Strip 3 - the end of this strip will go under the last orange strip.

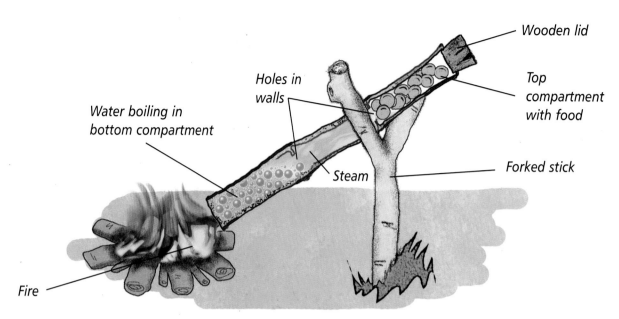

Water boiling in bottom compartment

Holes in walls

Wooden lid

Top compartment with food

Steam

Forked stick

Fire

A bamboo steamer for cooking

You may think that you couldn't cook the seafood you collected on an island without a metal object like a pan. If there is no metal on the island, but bamboo is growing, you can still make yourself a delicious hot meal. A bamboo stem is tall and strong. Some of the stem's strength comes from the way its inside grows. At intervals along the inside of the stem are thin woody walls, which give support. The positions of the walls can be seen as rings on the outside of the stem. The walls divide the stem into compartments, which can be used to make a bamboo steamer.

The steamer is made by cutting a length of bamboo with three compartments. The wall at one end is left in place, the wall at the other

end is removed, and a hole is made in each of the other two walls. Water is poured into the bottom compartment, and food is arranged in the top one. The bottom of the steamer is heated so that the water boils. Steam then rises through the bamboo and cooks the food. A wooden lid at the top of the bamboo stem slows down the passage of steam over the food, to help it cook.

Natural island materials have been used to build these village houses on one of the islands of American Samoa, in the Pacific Ocean.

A building made from island materials

For centuries, people who live on the islands of Samoa have built a type of house called a fale (pronounced far lay). The fale has a strong wooden framework and a thatched roof. The thatch is made from coconut palm leaves, woven together to make a rainproof sunshade. More palm leaves are used to make blinds, which can be raised and lowered on all sides of the building.

The fale floor is made from a layer of crushed dead coral, covered with more palm leaves. This provides a more comfortable and easy-to-clean surface than the sandy soil on which the fale is built.

As we are going to see, island weather can be windy, and at some times of the year **hurricanes** may blow over the island. In a hurricane, the fale has a big advantage over buildings with solid walls of brick and concrete.

When a hurricane is about to strike, a great difference in **air pressure** builds up between the outside and the inside of a building with solid walls. This difference in air pressure can cause the building to explode. This means that the walls of the building are pushed outwards and the building collapses.

The fale's more open structure of wood and palm leaves stops a difference in air pressure building up. This prevents the fale exploding and allows it to survive the hurricane.

Island weather

Islands that formed from volcanoes and coral are found in the warm seas and oceans around the equator. In this region the air temperature is high, so island weather is sometimes very hot. It is also affected by the way the winds blow.

Winds

Winds are produced by air flowing through the **atmosphere**. At the equator, hot air rises high into the sky and spreads out to the north and south. Eventually, it cools and sinks. Some of the air flows back to the equator. The rest of the air moves towards the poles.

If the Earth did not spin in space, the air would flow straight back to the equator or straight to the poles. In fact, the spin of the Earth makes the air

Many islands can have heavy showers at any time of year.

move in different directions, as the diagram shows. The winds that blow over the islands are called **trade winds**.

The different winds blow diagonally across the globe, either towards the equator or towards the poles.

Rain

Most winds that blow over islands travel a long way over seas and oceans too. As they do so, they take up water vapour from the water surface. The water vapour rises into the air and condenses to form clouds, which are carried along by the wind. When the wind and clouds reach an island, the air is forced upwards and becomes colder. More water vapour in the cloud condenses and the droplets become so large that they fall as rain.

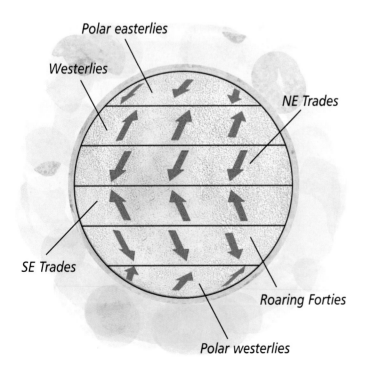

Polar easterlies

Westerlies

NE Trades

SE Trades

Roaring Forties

Polar westerlies

30

Looking for a weather pattern

Studying patterns in the weather helps people predict what kind of weather is on the way. For example, people on islands learn how to tell if a storm is coming. Scientists called meteorologists look for patterns in the weather and use them to make weather forecasts. You can look for weather patterns by using just two weather features – wind direction and air temperature.

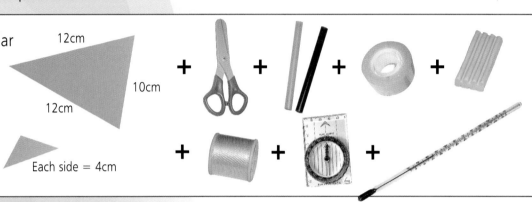

You need two triangular pieces of card, scissors, two plastic straws, sticky tape, modelling clay, a cotton reel, a compass, a thermometer.

12cm

10cm

12cm

Each side = 4cm

1 Make a simple wind vane as shown in the photo. Start by fixing the triangular pieces of card into slits cut at either end of a plastic straw. Next use modelling clay to fix one end of another straw to the middle of the first one. Put the lower end of the second straw through a cotton reel. Hold the cotton reel so the lower end of the straw rests in your palm. Your wind vane is ready for use.

Use sticky tape to hold the cards in place.

Use a lump of modelling clay to fix one straw to the other.

2 On several days when the wind blows, use your wind vane, compass and thermometer as follows and record your findings. Put the compass on a flat surface outside and find north and south. Hold up the wind vane and find the direction from which the wind is blowing. The arrow will point in this direction. Hold the thermometer in a sheltered place and take the temperature of the air.

Can you see a pattern, such as: When the west wind blows, the air is warmer?

Hurricane

In some parts of the oceans, groups of thunderstorms develop in very hot weather. Storm clouds are formed by huge amounts of hot air, filled with water. The clouds can be more than 10 kilometres tall. Ice crystals form inside them and are carried up and down on violently moving air currents. The ice crystals rub against each other and this makes electricity, which streaks through the cloud as lightning. The heat from the lightning makes the air **vibrate**, causing a roll of thunder.

After about a day, winds around the thunderstorms swirl them all together. In a few days they become one massive cloud, with a hole at its centre. This is a hurricane and the hole is called the 'eye'. Hurricanes are also known as cyclones or typhoons.

The hurricane's swirling winds push on the surface of the ocean and this make the water beneath the eye rise above its normal level, by up to 8 metres. The area of raised water is called the 'storm surge'. The winds close to the rim of the eye can travel round at 360 kph. Further away from the eye, but still under the clouds, the winds travel round at over 160 kph. To help you understand these wind speeds, think of a wind that blows an umbrella inside out: its speed is only about 45 kph.

A cross section of a hurricane

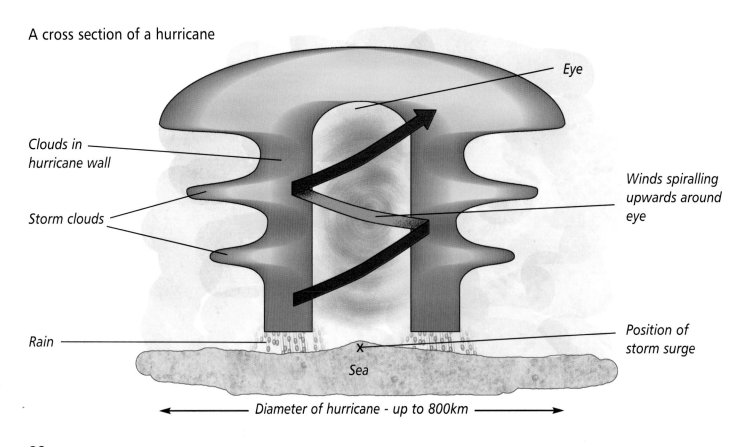

Eye

Clouds in hurricane wall

Winds spiralling upwards around eye

Storm clouds

Rain

Position of storm surge

Sea

← Diameter of hurricane - up to 800km →

A hurricane does not stay in one place. It moves across the ocean at about 50 kph. Hurricanes are tracked by satellites and information about them is given to people by television and radio. But if people do not have this help, they can tell that a hurricane is coming when they see several things happening. The size of the 'swell' (the normal rising and falling of the surface of the sea) increases. The sky at sunrise and sunset has many colours in it. Many feathery-looking clouds, called cirrus clouds, are blown by winds above the hurricane, and so they show its direction.

▼ *This photograph of the effects of a hurricane was taken in Apia, the capital town of Western Samoa.*

As a hurricane approaches an island, people should shelter in strong buildings or in caves or ditches. They should keep away from the beach, as the storm surge wave will sweep onto the land and cause widespread destruction.

When a hurricane strikes, the wind roars in one direction and causes great damage. Then there is about an hour when the air is calm, while the eye of the hurricane passes by. When the eye has moved on, the wind roars just as strongly in the opposite direction, until the rest of the hurricane has travelled past. People who have not found a place to shelter should simply lie flat, to avoid objects being flung around in the wind.

Island tides

On this beach on the island of Bermuda, you can see the wet sand left by the sea as the tide goes out. This beach could be at point X on the diagram below.

The sea laps on to the island beaches, sometimes bringing interesting and useful things with it. Twice each day, the sea moves further in over the beach than before. Then the sea moves out again. This happens because the level of the sea is constantly rising and falling. The reason for the rise and fall is **gravity**.

How the Moon's gravity influences the tides

The Moon's gravity pulls on the Earth and its oceans. This pull affects the oceans in the following way. The area of the ocean directly under the Moon is pulled the most strongly and the pull makes the water surface rise and form a bulge. On the other side of the Earth the pull acts to pull the ocean floor down and this makes a second bulge, as the diagram shows.

 The diagram shows a view of the Earth from the North Pole. Point X experiences changing tides as the Earth turns.

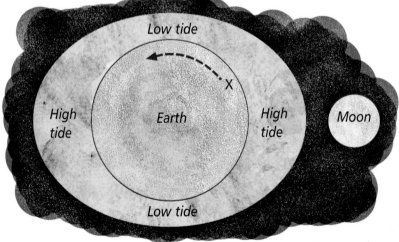

Every day the Earth spins on its **axis**, and so at different times of the day different parts of the seas and oceans are affected by the Moon. As a part of the Earth moves round towards one of the positions where it will be most directly affected by the Moon, the water level in that part of the Earth begins to rise. When the water reaches its highest level, it is said to be high tide.

As a part of the Earth turns away from one of the positions where it has been affected by the Moon, the water level falls again. When the water reaches its lowest level, and the sea is at its furthest from the beach, this is called low tide.

How the Sun affects the tides

Gravity exists between the Earth and the Sun, as well as between the Earth and the Moon. So the pull of gravity of the Sun also affects the Earth's tides. Over a month, the Moon moves round the Earth, and twice each month the Earth, Moon and Sun are in a line (diagrams a and c). At these times the Sun's pull of gravity and the Moon's pull of gravity work together, pulling very hard on the water. The water level on the Earth rises higher than at other times and the tides rise further up the beaches. These tides are called spring tides.

At two other times each month, the Sun and the Moon pull on the Earth from different directions (diagrams b and d). At these times the water level does not rise as much as usual, and the tides rise less far up the beach. These tides are called neap tides.

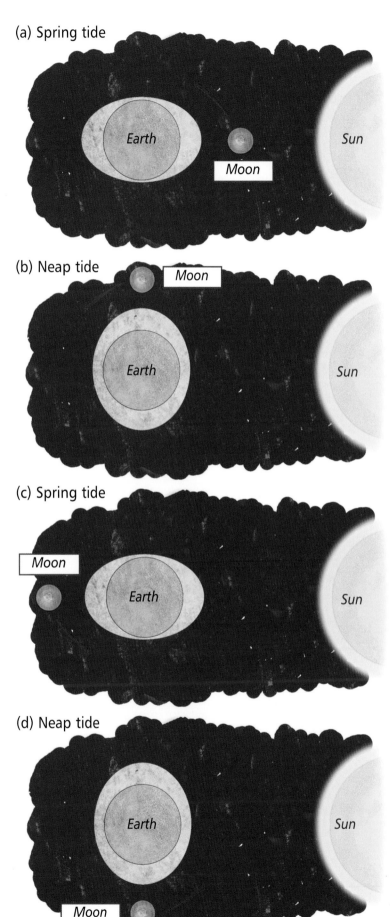

(a) Spring tide

(b) Neap tide

(c) Spring tide

(d) Neap tide

The danger of the tides

When the tide goes out, people on islands hunt for items left behind by the sea. They may find materials like cord, which can be used in making shelters. They may also collect food, such as clams or even seaweed. They need to take care that they don't get cut off by the water when the tide comes in again.

Ridges of sand may form across some sandy beaches and, at low tide, shallow pools are left in front of the ridges. People may wade through the pools and walk out over the ridges to the edge of the sea. Many of the shallow pools are connected by channels in the sand which run down the beach. When the tide comes in, water rushes up the channels and begins to fill the pools. If people by the sea's edge do not keep watch on the rising tide, they may find themselves cut off on a sand ridge.

Land does not always slope gently to the sea. Sometimes there is a high rocky cliff. At the bottom of the cliff, the pounding waves can knock holes in the rock called caves. People exploring the shore may see the caves, at low tide, and set out to visit them. If they do not take notice of the tide coming in, they may be cut off. The cave they thought of visiting may fill with seawater at high tide.

People trapped by the tides are usually rescued by boat or helicopter. The currents in the tide make it too dangerous for them to swim to safety.

These children are looking for seashells in the shallow water at low tide on an island in the Bahamas.

This is an artist's impression of a tsunami that hit the island of Java in 1883. It was caused by the eruption of a volcano called Krakatoa.

Tsunami – a dangerous wave

A **tsunami** is a giant wave of water. It can be made when an underwater volcano erupts or when there is an earthquake. An earthquake happens if the edges of two plates of the Earth's crust rub together, causing the rocks in the crust to shake.

Out in the open ocean, a tsunami may be hundreds of kilometres across but only between 30 and 60 centimetres high. However, the wave moves very fast – at 500 to 800 kilometres per hour. As it reaches land, it builds up into a wall of water over 30 metres high. This rushes up the shore, damaging everything in its path.

An earthquake that produces a tsunami may also be felt on islands in the region. Therefore, for people on an island, an earthquake can be a warning that a tsunami is on its way. If the force of an earthquake on an island is great enough to make a person grab something to hold onto, then a tsunami could follow. People should get onto high ground well away from a beach if they are to survive a tsunami.

An erupting volcano

Many island volcanoes are extinct, but some are dormant and may become active again. People need to know how to stay safe if the volcano starts to erupt.

A stream of red-hot lava looks threatening, but it is quite easy to escape from. Lava moves slowly, so people can run or just walk fast to get out of its way. However, some other dangers are caused by the eruption. For example, ash can form a thick cloud and the particles settle on everything. People caught in a cloud of ash must put a damp cloth over their nose and mouth. This acts as a **filter** to prevent the small rock particles entering their airways and lungs and damaging them.

As we saw on page 10, larger pieces of rock called blocks and bombs may fly through the air when a volcano erupts. They could cause severe head injuries. The best protection is a hard hat, like those used by workers on building sites.

Water vapour and other gases are released with lava. The water vapour condenses into water, and some of the gases dissolve in it, making acid water droplets. These form clouds and may fall as acid rain. People must cover their bodies to protect them from this type of rain, which damages the skin.

A huge ball of very hot gases may form at a volcano's vent. It spills out and rushes down the side of the volcano at over 100 kilometres per hour. If someone is in its path, they may be able to survive by diving into a pond or river and staying underwater while the gas ball passes over them.

The cloud of ash from an erupting volcano, like this one on the Caribbean island of Montserrat, can have a harmful effect on people's breathing.

Make a simple tilt machine

When a volcano is preparing to erupt, it swells up because of a build-up of pressure inside from the hot rocks. A tilt meter measures how much a volcano is swelling. The measurements are used to predict eruptions. You can make a model tilt machine to see how small changes can be measured.

You need card, scissors, sticky tape, white paper, modelling clay, thread about 12cm long, a drawing pin, a large book.

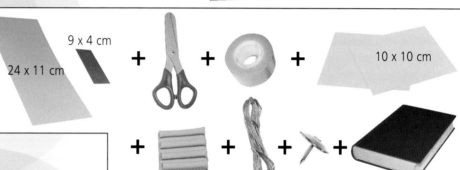

24 x 11 cm   9 x 4 cm   10 x 10 cm

1 Bend the larger piece of card. Cut the small piece of card in two, diagonally, and stick one of the pieces inside the bend of the large piece.

2 Make a scale on a square of white paper, by drawing one vertical line down the middle and more lines fanning out from the same point. Stick the scale to the front of the card.

3 Put a small piece of modelling clay on one end of the thread. Tie a simple knot in the other end and push the point of the drawing pin through the loop. Push the drawing pin into the top of the scale and card. The thread should hang down along the vertical line.

4 Put the tilt meter on the book and raise one end of the book. This represents the side of a volcano. Raise the book a little more. This represents the side of a volcano swelling. The thread hangs down different parts of the scale, depending on how much the book is tilted.

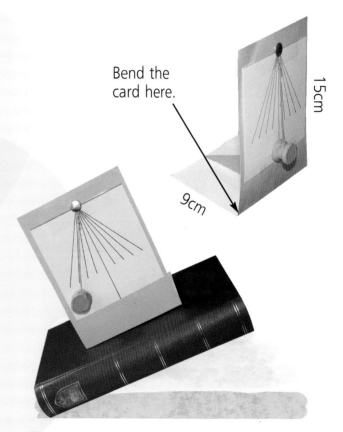

Bend the card here.

15cm

9cm

5 Make another scale with lines very close together. This measures even small changes in the tilt. It is a more accurate scale.

Protecting the skin

People exploring island beaches need to take special care to protect their skin from the Sun. The Sun does not just radiate light. It also radiates heat and **ultraviolet rays**. We can feel the heat rays, but the ultraviolet rays pass undetected into our skin. It is these rays which cause the skin damage that we call sunburn. Even on a cloudy day, on islands in a warm sea, large amounts of ultraviolet light may reach people on a beach.

People should not walk on coral reefs because this damages the coral. Also, the coral may cut their feet. If coral cuts the skin, small particles can get into the wound and become lodged there. The particles contain poison which they slowly release, causing pain. The wound with its coral pieces takes a long time to heal.

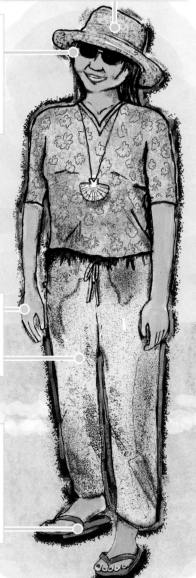

A wide-brimmed hat protects the head and neck.

Sunglasses protect eyes from the glare of the sand and the surface of the sea.

Clothes for a beach explorer

Clothes and sun-cream protect the skin from damage.

Shoes or sandals protect the soles of the feet from sharp fragments of coral.

Clothes that keep the skin covered are most comfortable for exploring forest areas, like this one in the Seychelles.

Away from the beach there may be areas of forest. Many of the plants have thorns to protect themselves, so island explorers need clothes that prevent them from being cut or scratched. It is best to wear long sleeves and long trousers. In the hot conditions, all wounds can easily become infected with germs and take a long time to heal.

Which cloth resists tearing the best?

Clothes for exploring the forest need to be made of material that does not tear easily. In this activity, you use the scientific method to help you find out which material would be most suitable.

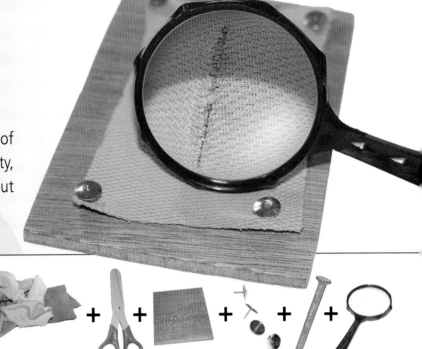

You need different types of cloth (e.g. cotton, wool, nylon, silk, linen), scissors, a piece of wood, four drawing pins, a nail about 5cm long, a magnifying glass.

1 Look at each type of cloth in turn and decide which you think will be best at resisting tearing.

2 Cut a piece from each material. All the pieces should be the same size (e.g. 6 x 4 cm).

3 Pin one piece onto the wood and drag the point of the nail across the cloth about 20 times.

4 Look at the cloth with the magnifying glass and record how much damage has been done.

5 Repeat steps 3 and 4 with each of the other pieces of cloth.

6 Put the pieces of cloth in order, starting with the one that resists tearing the best.

7 Which cloth would be best for making clothes for the forest?

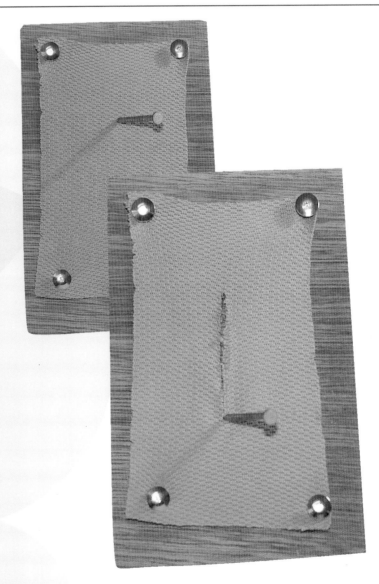

The danger of heat

Desert islands are hot, sunny places with damp or humid air. When people are exploring open country on the island, such as the old lava flows, they may forget how much the heat can affect their bodies.

When people walk or hike, their body muscles produce heat as they work. The Sun's rays shine down on their bodies, and more heat rays are reflected from the rocks. This makes conditions very hot. Normally, the body produces sweat to cool the skin and keep the body at its healthy temperature of 37ºC. But in extremely hot conditions, the body simply stops producing sweat, and its temperature rises to 41ºC. This makes the skin red. The pulse speeds up and thumps more strongly. A headache develops and the person may be sick and become confused and then unconscious. This illness is known as heat stroke. If treatment is not given, the person may die.

A person with heat stroke can be helped to cool down by resting them in the shade with their head and shoulders slightly raised. Their outer clothes should be removed and their skin should be sprinkled with tepid (only slightly warm) water. The person should also be fanned, to help cool them down, while others in the hiking party try to fetch medical help.

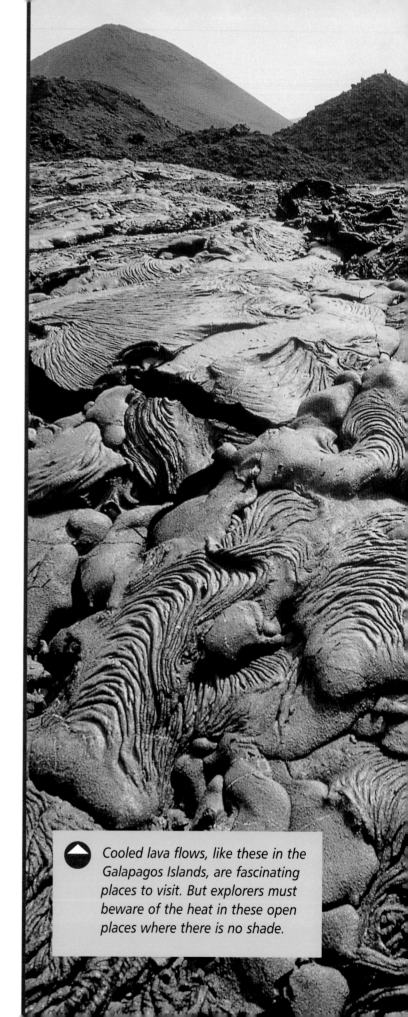

Cooled lava flows, like these in the Galapagos Islands, are fascinating places to visit. But explorers must beware of the heat in these open places where there is no shade.

Comparing fans

Do all fans produce the same amount of cooling or could there be a good design for heat stroke victims? Try this activity to find out.

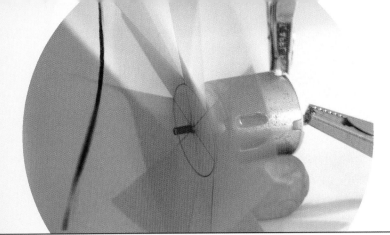

You need a motor, a battery, a switch, three wires covered in plastic, card, scissors, sticky tape, cotton thread.

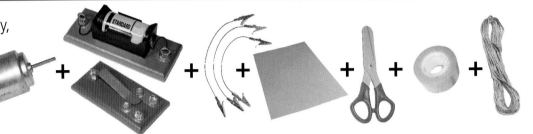

1 Set up the motor in a circuit, with the battery and switch. (See the photograph below.)

2 Close the switch to make sure that the motor works. Then open the switch again.

3 Design a circular fan on a piece of card.

4 Cut out the fan and twist the blades a little. Then stick the fan onto the motor with the sticky tape.

5 Close the switch and feel how the fan cools the skin.

6 Make and test other designs of fan, with more blades and fewer blades and blades of different shapes.

7 The coolness produced by the fan depends on how fast the air moves. Test each fan again by holding up a thread in front of it as it spins and noticing how much the thread is raised.

Bend the card a little on each blade.

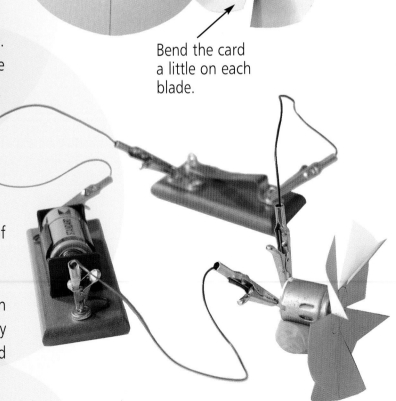

Rescue

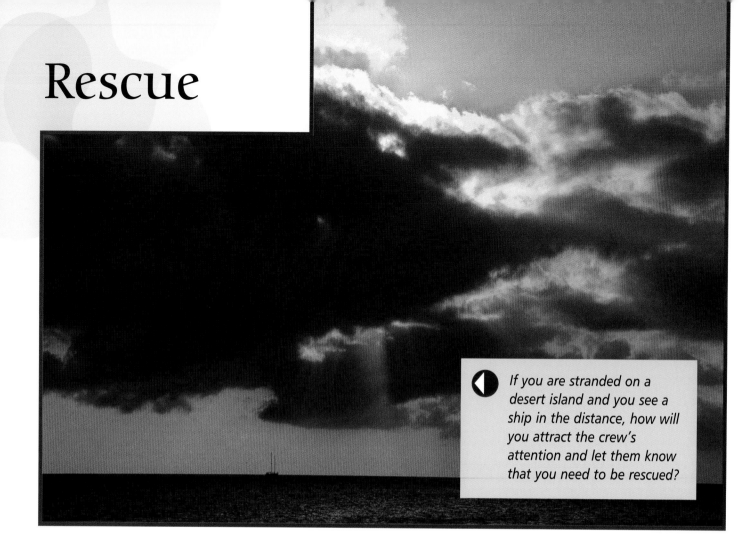

If you are stranded on a desert island and you see a ship in the distance, how will you attract the crew's attention and let them know that you need to be rescued?

If someone is marooned on a small desert island, they need to be rescued before they run out of food and water. They must find a way of showing other people that they are there.

Signal fires

A signal fire is simply a fire that is made to send a signal. If there is enough wood, three fires should be set up in the form of a triangle. Three is a number that people from many countries recognize as a signal of distress. If people in an aircraft or boat see three fires burning, a rescue party will be sent out.

The signal fires should not be kept burning all the time, or the supply of wood may run out. The fires should be made of very dry wood, and covered to keep off the rain. When an aircraft or boat is seen, the covers can be removed and the wood set alight. It will burst into flame quickly and produce a strong light that can be seen at a great distance, particularly at night.

Daytime signal

During the day, a highly reflective surface such as a mirror can be used to make three flashes at passing aircraft and ships. The flash is made by reflecting light from the Sun.

Warning!

If not in trouble, do not use a mirror to shine three flashes or any light at passing aircraft.

How is light reflected from a mirror?

To send a light ray from a mirror in a particular direction, you need to know how light is reflected.

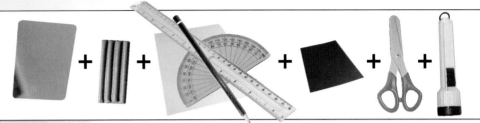

You need a flat mirror, modelling clay, paper, pencil, ruler and protractor, dark card, scissors, a torch.

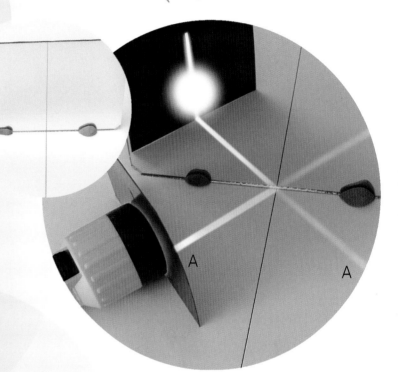

1 Use modelling clay to stand the mirror along one long edge of the paper. Draw a line from the centre of the mirror across the paper. The line should make a right angle with the mirror.

2 Cut a slit in a small piece of card and put it in front of the torch. Shine the torch at the point on the mirror where the line on the paper meets it.

3 Draw a line in the light ray from the torch and in the light ray reflected from the mirror. Label both lines A.

4 Move the torch and card and shine the torch so that its ray makes a different angle with the mirror. Repeat step 3 but label both lines B.

5 Switch off the torch, move it to a third position and draw lines where you think the rays will be. Switch on the torch to check your prediction.

The end of the journey

When people reach the end of a journey, they usually feel they have learnt a lot along the way. How did you get on, visiting the islands in this book? Can you explain how a hurricane forms or why a tilt meter can warn you of an erupting volcano? Also along the journey you have had many chances to try out your science skills of observing, predicting and experimenting. What did you discover? What would you do to survive if you were a castaway on a desert island?

Glossary

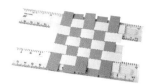

active   the condition of a volcano when it is erupting.

air pressure   the gentle push of the air on everything around it.

algae   tiny plant-like living things, which can only be seen clearly with a microscope.

atmosphere   the layer of gases which covers the surface of the Earth.

axis   an imaginary line through the Earth, from the North Pole to the South Pole.

bivalve   animal which has a soft body with two shells around it. The shells have a hinge and can open and close a little.

camouflage   a way of blending in with the surroundings, in order not to be seen.

colony   a group of animals which live closely together.

compost   a kind of soil made up from materials to provide all that seeds need to grow.

condense   change from a gas into a liquid.

coral reef   a ridge of coral that grows just below the surface of the sea.

crater   a huge bowl-shaped hollow in the surface of the Earth.

digest   break down food into small pieces so that the body can get nourishment from it.

digestive system   a part of an animal's body which digests food.

distil   separate a liquid from the substances dissolved in it by making it change into a gas and then condense again.

dormant   inactive. A dormant volcano may erupt again in the future.

driftwood   wood that has fallen into the sea and is carried by water currents until it is washed up on a beach.

erosion   a process in which weather conditions such as wind and rain break up rocky features, such as volcanoes and cliffs.

eruption   the release of lava, ash and gas from a volcano.

expedition   a journey which has a purpose, such as to study plants or rocks.

extinction   a process in which all of one kind of plant or animal die. It can also refer to the state of volcanoes which are no longer capable of erupting.

fertilizer   a substance containing materials called minerals, which plants use to help them grow.

filter	let a substance pass through a material with tiny holes, in order to separate any small solid particles in it.
friction	a force produced when two surfaces rub together.
fungicide	a substance that kills fungi such as moulds, which attack seeds.
granite	a rock which forms from hot rock that has cooled inside the Earth's crust.
gravity	the force that pulls objects down to the centre of the Earth. The Sun and Moon also have a force of gravity which pulls on objects around them.
hurricanes	storms with very high winds which develop in tropical regions. Seen from above, their clouds form a huge circle.
lagoon	an area of salt water surrounded by coral reef.
magma	molten rock that forms in the Earth's crust and the mantle beneath it.
molten	turned into a liquid as a result of getting warm or hot.
observation	studying the way something is, or the way in which something happens.
organisms	living things made from one or more microscopic structures called cells.

paralyse	make a living thing unable to move.
plates	huge slabs of rock which form the Earth's surface.
radioactive substances	substances that release rays of energy and tiny particles as they change from one material into another.
rainforest	a forest of tall trees and ferns which grows in warm, wet conditions.
species	a kind of plant or animal.
tentacles	long, soft, bendy or flexible projections from an animal's body.
trade winds	winds that blow near the equator.
transpiration	a process in which water is lost by evaporation from surfaces of a plant shoot, such as those of the leaves.
tsunami	a giant wave of water produced by a volcanic eruption or earthquake.
ultraviolet rays	rays made from waves of energy, which can damage the skin.
vent	the hole in the top of a volcano.
vibrate	shake to and fro.
water vapour	the gas form of water, produced when water evaporates into the air.

Index